Minecraft Farming

An UNOFFICIAL Kids' Guide

Percy Leed

Lerner Publications • Minneapolis

Lerner Publications Company
An imprint of Lerner Publishing Group, Inc.
241 First Avenue North
Minneapolis, MN 55401 USA

For reading levels and more information, look up this title at www.lernerbooks.com.

Library of Congress Cataloging-in-Publication Data

Names: Leed, Percy, 1968- author.
Title: Minecraft farming : an unofficial kids' guide / Percy Leed.
Description: Minneapolis : Lerner Publications, [2023] | Series: Lightning Bolt Books. Minecraft 101 | Includes bibliographical references and index. | Audience: Ages 6–9 | Audience: Grades 2–3 | Summary: "Mining, building, and crafting are important in Minecraft. So is farming! From growing crops and animals to building underground farms, readers will learn about the creative things they can do with their Minecraft farm"— Provided by publisher.
Identifiers: LCCN 2022006388 (print) | LCCN 2022006389 (ebook) | ISBN 9781728476735 (library binding) | ISBN 9781728478777 (paperback) | ISBN 9781728483382 (ebook)
Subjects: LCSH: Minecraft (Game)—Juvenile literature. | Agriculture—Juvenile literature. | Farms—Juvenile literature.
Classification: LCC GV1469.35.M535 L4456 2023 (print) | LCC GV1469.35.M535 (ebook) | DDC 794.8/5—dc23

LC record available at https://lccn.loc.gov/2022006388
LC ebook record available at https://lccn.loc.gov/2022006389

Manufactured in the United States of America
1-52254-50694-4/15/2022

Table of Contents

Minecraft Farming

Minecraft is a popular game. Players explore the *Minecraft* world and choose the way they play.

Building a farm is just one of the many things *Minecraft* players can do.

Mining, building, and crafting are all important in the game. So is farming. Farming helps players stay alive.

Building a Farm

Minecraft players need food to live. They build farms that crops and animals can grow on.

An underground farm

Players can build their farm in many places. They can build it inside, outside, or underground.

To build a farm, players need grass, dirt, seeds, and water. Players also need a place with lots of light so crops can grow.

Farms can have crops or animals or both.

These are some farming tools. Farming tools include shovels and hoes.

Players need tools for their farm. They may use a shovel to move dirt and a bucket to gather water. For an underground farm, they may use coal ore to create torches for light.

Players farm crops such as vegetables and wheat. They also raise animals such as chickens, cows, and pigs.

Players can raise many kinds of animals, including sheep.

Using the crops and animals from their farm, players can make foods like rabbit stew or pumpkin pie.

Farming to Survive

Minecraft players can choose to play in Creative Mode or Survival Mode. In Survival Mode, players have to work to stay alive.

A *Minecraft* player fights a mob.

Players also fight mobs in Survival Mode. Mobs can be attracted to farms.

For example, some crops such as mushrooms grow best in the dark, but mobs are attracted to darkness. Placing lit torches in the area will help keep mobs away.

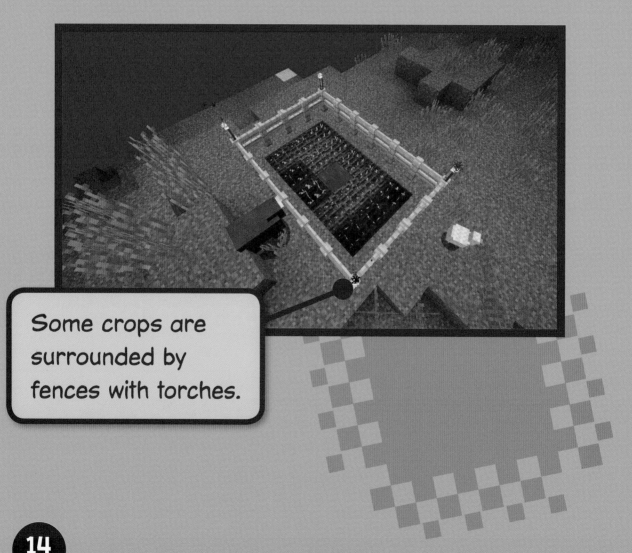

Some crops are surrounded by fences with torches.

Players look at their inventory screen to see what weapons or materials they have.

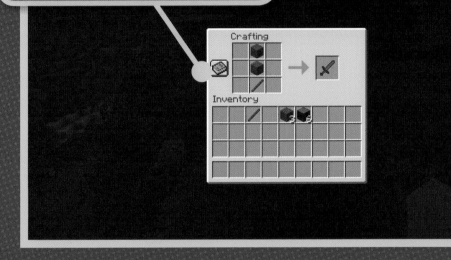

To protect their farm, a player needs to craft weapons. They can mine for the materials they need to make weapons, such as iron.

Creative Farming

Players get creative when farming in *Minecraft*. They can use mods to add things to their farm.

Mods can add new crops such as beans and beets. Mods can also add a new watering system that has hoses and sprinklers.

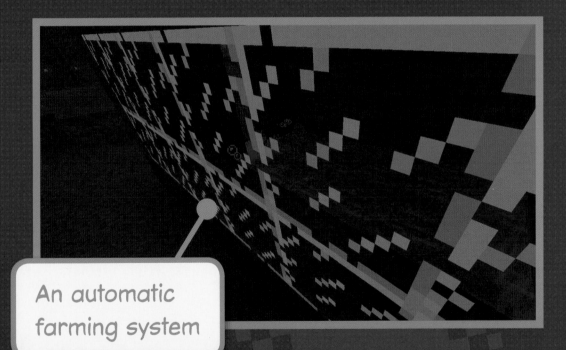

An automatic farming system

Players also use the *Minecraft* material redstone. Redstone is like electricity. Players can use it to create automatic systems.

This automatic system harvests crops so the player doesn't have to.

Automatic systems can do many tasks on a farm.

Automatic systems can water a player's crops and feed a player's animals for them. This saves a player time on farming. They can use this time to mine, build, and explore.

Minecraft is always growing and changing. And players will continue to try new things when farming.

A *Minecraft* player looks up from their farm.

Real-Life Farming

Automatic systems in *Minecraft* are similar to the systems used on real-life farms. Farmers use tools and technology to care for their crops and animals. Some tools check soil for moisture. This lets farmers know when to water crops. Other tools keep track of the health and safety of the animals on the farm.

Glossary

automatic: able to work by itself

craft: to make

Creative Mode: a freestyle, block-building mode in *Minecraft*

mob: animals and monsters in *Minecraft*

mod: code or instructions that computers can follow

Survival Mode: a *Minecraft* game mode where players must build, eat, battle mobs, and more to survive

system: a group of things that work together as a whole

Learn More

Gregory, Josh. *Mining and Farming in* Minecraft. Ann Arbor, MI: Cherry Lake, 2019.

Keppeler, Sam. *The Unofficial Guide to Using Tools in* Minecraft. New York: PowerKids, 2020.

Leed, Percy. Minecraft *Mining: An Unofficial Kids' Guide*. Minneapolis: Lerner Publications, 2023.

Minecraft Facts for Kids
https://kids.kiddle.co/Minecraft

Minecraft Official Site
https://www.minecraft.net/en-us

Minecraft Wiki: Farming
https://minecraft.fandom.com/wiki/Farming

Index

Photo Acknowledgments

Image credits: Various screenshots by Heather Schwartz, Linda Zajac, and Julia Zajac; omihay/Shutterstock.com, p. 4.

Cover: Linda Zajac.